A Bird's Nest

Nancy Hicer

Rosen REAL READERS

Rosen Classroom™
New York

Birds build nests.
This bird is looking for a place to build a nest.

The bird finds a place
to build.
She will build a nest
in this tree.

The bird finds grass
and sticks.

The bird brings the grass
and sticks to the tree.
She builds the nest.

She lays eggs
in the nest.
Baby birds will hatch
from the eggs.

The baby birds hatch.

They are hungry.

The mother bird leaves the nest
to find food.
She looks for worms
in the grass.

She finds worms.

The babies will eat the worms.

The mother bird brings worms to the nest.

She feeds the baby birds.

The baby birds grow up.
They leave the nest.
Someday they will build
their own nests.

Words to Know

bird

eggs

nest

sticks

tree

worms